BETWEEN THE DOORPOSTS

BETWEEN THE
DOORPOSTS

ISA MILMAN

Ekstasis  Editions

National Library of Canada Cataloguing in Publication

Milman, Isa
    Between the doorposts / Isa Milman.

Poems.
ISBN 1-894800-45-1

        I.†Title.

PS8576.I5743124B48 2004   C811'.6   C2004-901512-5

Author photo: Robert McConnell
Cover art: *Israel on Fire #3,*
        monoprint by Isa Milman, 2001, private collection

Edited by Patrick Lane

Published in 2004 by:
Ekstasis Editions Canada Ltd.   Ekstasis Editions
Box 8474, Main Postal Outlet   Box 571
Victoria, B.C. V8W 3S1   Banff, Alberta ToL oCo

Between the Doorposts has been published with the assistance of grants from the Canada Council for the Arts and the British Columbia Arts Council administered by the Cultural Services Branch of British Columbia.

For my mother,
Sabina Kramer Milman

and in memory of my father,
Eliyahu Milman, 1914-1997

"How can one take delight in the world unless one flees to it for refuge?"

Franz Kafka

CONTENTS

INTRODUCTION

One of my earliest memories is my mother teaching me the *Kriyat Shema*, after she tucked me into bed. Every night I'd recite this prayer as old as the Jewish people: "Hear O Israel, the Lord is our God, the Lord is one. And you shall love your God with all your heart, with all your soul, with all your being. Set these words upon your heart, and teach them to your children. Talk of them in your home, and when you are going on your way; when you lie down, and when you awaken. Bind them as a sign upon your hand; let them be a symbol before your eyes, and inscribe them on the doorposts of your house, and on your gates…"

This prayer, written on parchment, is slipped into a little case that's affixed to the doorposts of Jewish homes, so that we'll remember. It's called a *mezzuzah*, which in Hebrew means doorpost.

Another early memory is asking my mother where were our grandparents. I don't really remember a moment of asking this, it's more a feeling of my mother's anguish and how my being floated in it. We floated together in this ocean of loss, and over time, she told me her stories.

This collection of poems is about my living in between. My identity and my place in the world as a Jew, my attachment and longing for my murdered family, and my growing up in North America, trying to not dwell in the past. It's also about gratitude for the fantastic gifts of my life. And always, my struggle with God: I am not a believer. I believe.

Isa Milman
December 2003

BETWEEN THE DOORPOSTS

Before I Was Born

I had the brightest to choose from
I come from a gorgeous line.

The rabbis gathered round, coaxing me,
their tenderness a surprise, but I had
reason to be afraid.

What did it matter, beauty,
to be spat upon, torn to pieces, buried alive.
I knew what happened to my cousin Mordechai.

Look at my sooty self-portrait, how my features
are missing, how I begged for more time.

Mother spent her days crying,
the porch door banged in the wind.

They told me I wouldn't remember,
promised good times, an ocean-crossing,
be a girl.

I was tired, my grief as complete as a
continent, face puffy as a cloud.

HEBREW LESSON

language is a very difficult thing to put into words
Voltaire

In the beginning there's *aleph*, the alpha, numero uno, the *a*
but why start here,
let's begin with *chai*
a simple word composed of two letters, *chet* and *yod*
please don't say chet, as in Baker,
say *het*, as if about to softly clear your throat,
slightly deeper than a *huh* sound, now add *eh*, and close it with *t*,
that's it, *chet*
yod is easier to say, and when written, it's not much bigger than a
point,
but don't underestimate it,
it's the first letter of God, and origin of *Yid*,
but that's another lesson.

chai is basic, it's life. Usually expressed in its plural,
and when preceded by *lamed*, we're lifting our glass, singing,
to life, to life, l'chaim with fiddlers serenading dairy cows
as they fly over the stetl's bright moon.

Chaim is also a name, for males of the species.
For females, its *Chaya*, which can also mean creature,
or beast. My mother liked to call me *wilde chaya*,
and she called my sisters this too. O America, what it did to us.

But back to the *yod*. Remember it's a tiny letter,
so sometimes it's stretched into a *vov*,
to look like *yod's* longer version. This is reserved
for special occasions, as in the case of Eve.
Her original name is *Chava*, which is *Chaya* with a *vov*,
man's name for the mother of all living. Would you believe
this little stretch continues to distinguish the *he* from the *she*,
which in Hebrew is the *who* and the *he*,
but let's do pronouns another time.

So how does Chava become Eve? It helps to know that
vowels are dots and dashes sprinkled around letters,
but they never appear in the Torah text.
You either know the word, or you guess.
How could a monk pronounce the pesky *chet*,
the easy *vov*, the silent *hey*?
Eve makes sense in translation.

MY FAMILY LIFE

always a challah for Shabbos
always soup with dinner
always Saturday night dairy
always Nantasket Beach
always Filene's Bargain Basement
always too many clothes in the closets
always squeezed between sisters
always Maimonides Yeshiva
always Blue Hill Avenue
always the absent grandparents
always my father driving
always my mother working
always the aerograms from Israel
always what's on the news
always the goyim, the goyim, the goyim
always Mummy's memories
always Daddy's silence
always be a good girl
always stay away from those boys
always remember
always light the candles
always Jewish calendars
always Pesach, Rosh Hashanah and Yom Kippur
always Yiddish
always Isele, Esterel, Eveniu
always go do your homework
always it's your turn to do the dishes

STOLIN

Try to praise the mutilated world.
Remember June's long days,
and wild strawberries, drops of wine, the dew.
The nettles that methodically overgrow
the abandoned homesteads of exiles…

                    Adam Zagajewski

My father dreams of Stolin,
as he rides the giant tractor in the Siberian taiga.
He worries for his mother, sister, brother.
Have the Nazis already come?
He is a prisoner, five thousand miles from home.

Yesterday I found him in a photograph
dwarfed by the machine, and mother,
who remembers everything, can't say
how this picture came to be.

She was his godsend and he saved her life,
he liked to claim. This is how fate works its surprises,
how the days of his sentence for a crime never named
stretched into years. Then without warning
more rumbling on another train of exile from tundra
to desert, the roof of the world.

I tell this story to a lover, long ago.
We're sitting on my balcony,
on a boozy Montreal eve. I'm showing him my atlas,
along with lots of leg, tracing my parents' journey
through pages cluttered with the cross-hatch
of mountains. I find Fergana, explain how
grapes grew big as ladies' fingers,
and pomegranates were squeezed for the juice.
We are thirsty. We like how our tongues feel
when we say Uzbek, *crepuscule.* The sky is purple.
We are about to kiss.

People ask where I'm from, and I wonder how far back to go,
how to explain that *Stolin* means all that is forever lost, but remains,
in the dark shapes of absent loves that visit me, in dreams:
war is again brewing on the roof of the world,
my parents are tumbling across continents.

SEARCHING FOR WALLENBERG

My name is Vera. I work for Raoul.
He disappeared after Budapest and
my job is to find him.

In the Gulag you'll find no wild game but
many have lost teeth biting into
a wolf. When there is no cutlery
such things are possible. Why, one night,
as I hurried from commissary to hut,
through knee deep snow
I was forced to throw hot soup
in a wolf's face.

My name is Vera. I cannot find Raoul.
My cookbook was a modest success.
How to Cook a Wolf did not appeal to California.
It is possible to substitute ingredients, but of course
the taste can go sour. I prefer beets.
Such a lovely colour plus a little rose for the toilet.
There's no colour for winter. We must invent.

My name is Vera. I've been forced to uproot.
I'm banned from travel; my books have been
pulled from the shelves of kitchens. Still not a word
from Raoul. He was seen scratching letters
in a wall in Lubyanka, so they say.
We have no proof.

Lubyanka sounds nice, so feminine.
Like Treblinka. I know, it's so rude of me
to bring it up. What's in a name, you say.

Mama, Isaac and Me

I.

No, Mama, I wasn't surprised when you found my old *chumash* in
the cellar last summer, pages bonded together by mold. Saving
things is what you live by. Look around your house: the shrine in the
dining room bulging with gold-leaf china you bought with German
money, the diamond earrings, pearls, ruby brooches, wrapped in tis-
sues, muffled against silver dollars, stuffed in pockets of dresses from
Filene's Basement, circa 1965...
Yes of course I'm attached to these things—I made you promise me
the needlepoint of Isaac, looking like a girl with curls, bewildered, his
cheeks flushed, the ram grazing innocently in the background—who
could believe in the slaughter?

II.

I took off at seventeen, with your blessing, to *eretz hakodesh*, where
you always dreamed of living, but the war there freed me for my
own wildness. Scrubbing off your past like dried blood from healing
skin, I flew to San Francisco. Remember my phone call that summer
of love? You weren't home, so I left a message, about my wedding on
Potrero Hill.

III.

Such a bitter birth I gave you, at least I could have been a son.
Even that small joy denied you, like a last kiss from your parents,
watching behind the wire, as the train took you to the Gulag.

You named me after Yitzhak, your father,
hushed me to sleep singing *Numah b'ni*,
you called me Tateleh
          Iseleh
          Iseniu
          Isulka,
            sleep in peace, my little son,
            don't cry, Mama's right here,
            protecting you from all harm...
I was a quiet child.

Family History

Imagine—
they lived on this earth but were forbidden to leave a trace

Imagine—forbidden to leave a trace

but I'm here with no choice but to tell you

how Yelena flipped pancakes while holding a book in her other
hand, because there was never enough time to read

how Sabina and Yitzhak would sing *a capella*,
and the neighbours were grateful for their gifts

how they worried about making ends meet with five daughters
and no money since the mill burnt down

how Basia published poems when she was 14 and she received a letter
saying: *the crown of the poet belongs on your head*

how the twin sisters left Kostopol for Warsaw to study
and Basia married Pesach
and Sabina married Olek
for love was burning

how Sabina escaped from Warsaw while the bombs were dropping,
and Olek was arrested by the Russians and Sabina went with him to
Siberia

how they sent Pola, Miriam and Sonia off on a train to who knew
where they would end up

how they stayed behind hoping that the worst was already past,
but it was only just beginning

and how Basia and Pesach had a son called Mordechai

and how they were forced to watch as Pesach was beaten to pieces

and how Yitzhak died that night of a shattered heart

and how Mordechai was two years old when he was buried alive

and how Yelena and Basia starved in the ghetto
until they were forced
to dig their own grave in the football field

forbidden to leave a trace

 And I repeat:
        Yitgadal veyitkadash shemey rabah

and I ask:
        make me a channel of your peace;
        where there's despair in life, let me bring hope;
        where there is darkness only light;
        and where there's sadness, ever joy...

PSYCHIATRY WARD, ST. MARY'S, MONTREAL

I thought I could cure anything

with compassion

and the working of the hands

discovered meditation and

non-doing

believed my rescue kit was full

just breathe and let mind be

mind is the family graveyard,

the final resting place is me

Two Letters After a Visit: A Poem in Three Voices

this morning I found Jaffa's note. She had to leave so early,
didn't want to wake us,
so she wrote,
>Dear Isa and Robert
>thank you so much for last night
>a fabulous meal with dear dear friends

she'd written on the blank side of some paper she'd found on my
desk. Curious, I flipped it over, to find something I'd saved three
years ago (didn't have the stomach to read it then). An email from
Murray in Windsor (internet friend) re: Stolin (my father's home
town)
>*you may find this interesting…from my uncle*
>*a letter dated January 11, 1946:*
>*Today is the luckiest day of my life.*
>*That is how I felt upon reading a letter*
>*written in my brother's hand.*
>*How many days and nights have I thought of only one*
>*thing. Will you ever know of the dark fate which befell us?*

Better go back to Jaffa's note, I decide, taking a breath:
>A real sense of belonging (which I've missed)
>feels like coming 'home' again
>I slept really well, I always do in that bed,
>and woke realizing how much I miss being around you both
>give little Emily a kiss from me

Sweet. Thank you Jaffa dear friend. Now Murray, finally, here goes:
>*we had to wear yellow stars, even children in the crib.*
>*You can't imagine how I felt when our sister's children*
>*were all beastly raped. Our little Chava, 14 years old.*
>*Their eyes when they look at me. And I am helpless. Might*
>*as well be dead. When somebody died we didn't mourn. We*
>*said at least they will not suffer*

until the ill-fated day before Rosh Hashana, 7000 people
lived in the ghetto of Stolin. We dug our own graves.
Everything was planned ahead. All disrobed first, led to
the graves and shot. Hundreds buried alive. Father said his
prayers looked at me with beautiful sad eyes. Like he begged
I should forgive him for bringing me into this world.
Mother washed herself. Said prayers was ready to die:
    Leave us, leave us, you must remain alive

BURGERKINDER 1925

a fiction from a photograph by August Sander

They're holding hands, watching the camera bellows
and its cyclops eye. Herr Sander stoops behind
a black cloth, coaxing them to feel free,
but to stay very still, and of course
they can't feel free, so they hold hands.
With their eyes like chestnuts,
with their round faces, they could be twins.
They're in a German city,
maybe Munich, maybe Hanover, maybe Berlin.
It's 1925. They're in their best clothes, her dress
is ruffled, his white shirt spotless,
their boots polished.
We could give them names, she could be Gerda,
he, Helmut, and guess that she is seven
and he is eight.

We could believe that their mother
is a worrier, who demands cleanliness above all,
no dust on her furniture, no garbage
in her kitchen, no pets, *Ach so much dirt.*
We can hear her yelling at Rosa to hurry up
with the potatoes, that she's lucky to have work
and food, because Herr Stein is a generous man,
even though his head is always filled with accounts,
but when he comes home he likes his schnapps
and his Beethoven, then a kiss from Helmut and Gerda
before their bath and bed.

We can wonder how this family has prospered
seven years since the war. We could say it's their
munitions factory, or perhaps their flour mill,
but it doesn't really matter. We could think
that Helmut and Gerda always squabbled.
She would say: *Mutter, please, for my birthday,*
a chocolate butter cake dusted with sugar
like the snow soon to fall, and Rosa would drop her knife
and run to the market to bring home the eggs and cocoa,
and a metre of taffeta for a new dress.

Looking in Helmut's eyes, we can see his childhood
flicker by, we can watch him chase marbles, careful not to
crawl under porches, or kneel in the dust of summer streets.
We can hear his boots squeak their newness in the company
of thousands of marching feet. Let's wonder at
his willingness, and pity his death
in the snows of Stalingrad,
while Gerda waits for news.

My Life in Theatre

I tumble down an escalator in the Port Authority Bus terminal
carrying a Samsonite case in each hand. Someone helps me
to my feet. I'm meeting Cheryl but she's not there. I guess
her audition's going longer than planned.

Bob comes over to my table at the Café Finjan. He hands me
some matches, opens with a line: did you know that tactile stimuli
create synaptic complexity, enabling such marvels as the sprouting
of dendrites or the capacity to speak the language of dogs?

Back in Boston I prefer the stairs. Cheryl has to move, so
we pack her belongings and drive to New York.
Try parking a U-Haul trailer on Columbus. Talk about
steamed-off cabbies and the neighborhood dogs out of control.

Cheryl flies to Paris. She's learning *commedia dell'arte* from
Jacques LeCoq, the mime. I sit in Bob's place, peering into the mirror
of my Samsonite. Fresh from the shower, Bob approaches
from behind. Try as I might I cannot turn around.

Cheryl writes that she's got a role on StarTrek.
I should come and visit in L.A.

I'm living in Paris, in a seventh floor walk-up, *chambre de bonne,*
with a turkish toilet outside my door. The matchbook falls out
of my vanity. *Your answers lie inside you,* it observes.
I see Bob's cock framed neatly in the mirror. I've lost his address.

I've had it with Paris, even though I like to watch
those twig brooms sweeping dog shit into gutters,
while I smoke Gauloises in cafés. I go to study brain slices
in a lab in Montreal, wishing Cheryl all the best in L.A.

ABOUT *Story 1964*

Robert Rauschenberg created Story 1964 *during a*
performance of Story.
Merce Cunningham: My choreography has no story

His smears, rags, scraps of wood, and metal,
paper cut-outs of peas and oranges,
images once stuck to billboards flogging beer, tv dinners
make me zing
as if the sun, moon, stars and planets
are handling every molecule of my body
just enough to let me know
that I too belong
that a space is reserved for me
despite Hitler and Stalin and Pol Pot and bin Laden

that the racket in my brain urges me to make a big mess
and remember
crushed insects yield red cochineal,
egg-yolks bind pigment tighter than glue
ochre and sienna come from stones,
and Rauschenberg comes from New York

remember I once slicked my body in oil
and danced 'contact'
naked in an Amherst back yard
with Steve and Debbie and Nita and Kurt
because we were children of Merce Cunningham
and it was 1972, high summer

THREE FLYING SONGS

1.

The first time,
seventeen,
in a trim white suit.
On my own
to the Holy Land,
I refuse to lower
the blind.

Stepping down
in dusty yellow Lod,
too shy to kneel,
I kiss the ground
in my mind.

2.

Zurich layover,
I'm in a line.
Turn around
to his shocking
blue eyes.
No it was
my eyes, he said.
It was fate,
he said.
On the same flight
to Montreal,
we couldn't stop
our reckless tongues.

3.

Daddy died last night,
alone.
Alone,
Victoria to Miami,
clouds surround this metal capsule.
His body empty now
is he just light?

Wet Dog Day

Nobody stuffs the world in at your eyes
if your attention is elsewhere, when you're
taking your dog for her appointment, say,
for a complete hysterectomy, and it's Thursday,
a rainy day in October. You won't notice
the smell of wet leaves decomposing (you have refrained
from the rake once again. obedient wife)

the day doesn't remind you of the time you climbed a small mountain
in New Hampshire, with Jim Stamoulis— dear edge-pusher, love-poet,
teaser; you scaredy-cat in your suede hiking boots
don't register the weight of damp air, of your legs lifting

                              (Maggie pulls hard on her leash)

you are in yellow birch leaves vibrating against a gunmetal sky,
not remembering how you wanted to inhale those colours,
feel them fill your lungs, enter your bloodstream

and hum to you, a chant that you would memorize,
and teach your children (when you have them)
along with *Shehecheyanu*, your favorite prayer,
thanking God for creating us
and bringing us
to this moment.

D. T. G.

for Malachy

Secret message of my bathrobe's monogram
decoded one Sunday morning circa 1992.
You were resting your thumbs from tetris,
and you were such a whiz. I was jealous,
I admit it. Those shapes I couldn't
for the life of me
turn fast enough to even score.
Hey Mom, what do those initials stand for?
Don't Take Gumph made you giggle.
Chalk one up for Mom.

You agreed to hold hands
walking home from Westmount pool,
and I made sure to store that touch
for future reference—guess we both knew
we'd have precious few more

Your autograph was still embedded in the sidewalk.
Lucky you when you found that fresh cement.
And such high profile—the only Malachy around.
I'm glad your name feels good to you,
even though it's a pain for others to pronounce.

It hit me hard last night,
when you told me you hadn't
even met Maggie yet,
or your niece Emily—
can it be three years
since you've been home?

Got me thinking you're the one
that's always petting Crowley in the photos,
and I flashed on the time we had such a blast
discussing Mark Strand's "Great Dog Poem No. 2"
for your English project, senior year. Wish we'd had
more of that, but you were in such a hurry
to move on, and I don't blame you,
I was like that too.

But those deep black holes of absence
I just don't understand. Been reading up
on the male cortex, though, and sure enough,
we've got such different brains. Gotta throw
all that 'gender is but a social construct' dogma
out the window. I was stuck on that big time
when I was going to school.

You're learning all this in your courses, *n'est ce pas*,
but let's be honest—what good is all that research
if you're still not inspired to reach for the phone.

I promised I'd come to your graduation,
and I'm looking forward to it, really,
I can hardly wait. Then you'll come back for a visit,
and going for a walk down Cook Street, we'll ...*look within
and bark, and look at the mountains down the street
and bark at them as well...*

FOUR SONGS ABOUT LAUNDRY

At Ways Mills, I stood on a stool at the corner of the porch
pinning the sheets and towels on the line
while the kids got lost in the grass behind the house
or lolled on the beat-up sofa
watching the baler drop its parcels
around the neighbour's fields.
I loved hanging out the wash.
The wind whipped the sheets dry in two minutes flat.
I was infatuated then, writing the guy letters
about the landscape, how it was lifted from a Renaissance
painting. He stopped writing back.
Folding the sheets, I'd bury my nose in fresh wind
startled by happiness

•

At the hospital she told me to forget about cooking.
She'd had a lifetime of it, the hours put into something
devoured in a blink. *I'll take laundry any day,*
sometimes it even lasts a week. And the ironing

•

First, the collar, pay special attention to the points.
Be careful at the shoulders. Creases aren't allowed.
Soothe the cloth with those boy-stroking hands,
then do the sleeves,
both sides

Stout breasts cosied in aprons
kibbutz-lady lessons
I'd never forget

·

You put on Pavarotti or Te Kanawa
take your heap of bruised and mangled cloth
spray some linden water, and apply heat
with a firm and steady hand —
give me an iron and I'll press with my life

Love, in Hiding

for Jan

In Rotterdam, they sheltered in his greenhouses,
sleeping close to the roots of rhododendrons:
the strains of your father's imagination.
By day, they ate at his table
while you and the other children soaked
your bread alongside. After curfew
you would steal across the water
to where the weapons lay hidden,
alert, having already buried friends.

These things you told me amid crystal
and silver, in a place where attentive waiters
whisked crumbs off crisp linen,
and we dressed with care.

I loved the father you gave me, the one
who pinned his star inside his breast pocket
and harboured strangers marked for death,
in greenhouses, where he taught you
how plants eat light, drink water,
and survive.

Chance brought you to make me a garden,
where I spent days obsessed in your past.
Many nights I took off my clothes and waited
for you, to take me back there, in my flesh.

But unlike your father, you were afraid to risk.
You kept me hidden, rarely inviting me in
for a meal. For a year my heart strained
against my containment. But enough.
Hunger opened my mouth,
taught me to speak.

Remembering Ray

Ray is dead
I hear a string of words
Dinner is cooking
the kids are doing homework upstairs
the phone's at my ear and
I'm riding the luge
down memory's run

We're at *l'Express* on St. Denis
the kids are drinking Shirley Temples
dressed for Halloween,
the last time we saw him he was

such a handsome Georgia boy,
ran from the law to escape Viet Nam,
a Southern boy who lived French,
dated Nina Simone. I didn't know
too many Southern boys, didn't know
the half of his addictions,
alcohol, tobacco, cocaine,
grief for a Daddy who died too young like

Ray. Ray is dead
Dinner is cooking
I'm gripping the sofa,
knocked by each breath into

his 'pink house' near Carré St. Louis,
we're emptying a closet-full of *New Yorkers*
to make refuge for me and the kids,
while February seizes my breath
and I can't stop crying

We never took that trip to Florence. We stopped kissing
on my balcony, stopped
touching before the last touch was too many

Remember now the year
I moved up from Boston,
the man I would marry saying to me,
come here darling, there's someone
you just have to meet

Dinner is cooking
the kids are setting the table.
His voice was faint and woozy
the last time we spoke,
we were making a date
to catch up on missing years
but we never did

Ray is dead
The news is a string of words

LAKE OF TWO MOUNTAINS

for Robert

Take the way we met. What fiction
were we creating
floating in that salty pool?
You told me about the whale that slid
right under your boat in the kelp bed.
I remember we couldn't let go.
How we awoke with hand cleaved to hand,
like your tongue to the floor of your mouth
on the day you were born.

Now your tongue glides with grace like
a boat cutting through grassy water.
Even in winter, freedom lends you heat
but good as you are at loving
the fear is real.

You were going to get the firewood
alone, but changed your mind. Outside,
a snowy cabin is perched above an icy lake.
My hands are sheltered in yours,
as we watch a sky heavy with stars
slide behind a whale-white moon.

First Peony of the Season

for Anna

I bring it in
to watch it unfold
while I do the dishes

Yesterday your flight left so early
you never had time to say
good-bye to the garden

I took your birthday dress
from the closet,
saw you in your ten-year-old body
radiant in Provencal colours
that swirled like illuminated script

The peony fattens on the counter,

your dress, draped over my
bedframe, lights up the dark

CORVETTE DREAMING

Daddy drives like a man alone.
His Thunderbird swoops from lane to lane
without a backward glance, stop signs
glide smoothly by, complaints pass unheard.
He is Paul Newman in *Exodus*
nothing can stop him.

His car is full of trash, but he doesn't seem to mind,
doesn't notice the many pairs of worn-out
running shoes in the back seat, his empty
soda bottles, stale lunches, old papers and tools—
tidiness is mother's domain.
But how he hates his own untidiness—
that shunted vein in his wrist, bulging
like a giant worm trapped in a tunnel,
so the tubes can plug in easily, less fuss.
He doesn't agree to it for the longest time, stuffs
cotton in his ears when the doctors come to discuss it.

In the hospital he sits three days a week, watching his blood
arc through crimson loops and rush back
freshly laundered. Dressed always in long sleeves,
he still dreams of a red Corvette, payback for his youth
stolen by a Europe that ate him alive. Ever the speed-loving
glamour-boy, his girls grown up and long-gone,
nurse-mother weighs and measures everything—
two ounces of potato, a sliver of herring, a few drops of beer.

I remember his doctor saying he wouldn't last long
if they took his license away, even after he got lost near home
and clocked a hundred miles trying to find his way.
Mother, hysterical, tried to take away his keys, but
he was wise to her. Besides, he'd bought a little red car
that was waiting for him at the used-car lot.

That night she phoned us, we came as quickly as we could.
Thud of dirt from my shovel the sound of our farewell,
and the next day, the hospital clerk handing me
the plastic bag with his wallet, watch and clothes.
She seemed accustomed to the wild moaning from my lips.
I would have given anything to kiss him good-bye.

WAKING UP

I would like to give you the silver
branch, the small white flower;
a wet hankie of truce. But most mornings,
I wake to find little shards of hatred
in a corner— the broken
dishes, my houseplants tossed out the window,
your handprint on my cheek—
it must be thousands, the days
that have been soiled by remembering.

The card I sent you, of a man
on a tight-rope, one end anchored,
the other, in his own hand,
as he walks out his window
into the night sky,
you returned, the envelope marked
'unexamined'.
I had thought you were dying.

Picking up the old jasmine's discarded leaves
this morning, I discovered its first tiny
blossom, sweet joy rising up my nose.

Go on, go on, wake up.

FOR THE RECORD

she likes to make lists, like the books she brought for the ride
from Victoria to Nelson in 2002: Nabakov's *Speak Memory*,
David Grossman's *Sea Under Love*
and the *Best American Poetry 1998*, with Donald Hall's
"Letter" to Jane Kenyon after she died, that made Nira cry
when she read it to her in Brookline last Spring

she thinks it matters to write things down, as if some day
someone will pore over her papers and say,
look here, she loved Rauschenberg, Merce Cunningham
and Joseph Cornell,
rode across the Brooklyn Bridge in a limo with Twyla Tharpe,
saved every card and letter that passed through her mailbox,
and had dates with the man on the postage stamp
but only bragged about it to her close friends

she admires Bob and Joan from next door,
who kept a diary of their every day
and when uncertain about the town where they rode elephants
in Burma, or the meal they ate in St. Petersburg, or the month
the wood-tits visited their red-laquered spirit-house in the garden,
they could just look it up

and she wishes she were more disciplined,
like the man in New Jersey she read about,
who detailed his unremarkable life in thousands of notebooks
causing a bidding war amongst urban anthropologists
who recognized the value of the documents,
because it's all in the details

but then she remembers the words of Jack Kornfield,
speaking of what matters at the end of life:
did I live well? did I love well? was I kind?

HANGING THE STAR OF DAVID ON BLANSHARD STREET
for Jack Gardner

At the 'Bereavement as Healing' conference in Montreal
the woman was shocked to see a *Mogen David* around my neck,
surely no shield, no protection on the streets of Paris
where she hid as a child. *Aren't you afraid*
to show yourself as a Jew?

I grew up with fear, as familiar to me as my own bed,
as the sound of my parents breathing in the next room.
After my *kriyat shema*, my prayer before sleep,
the stars were always yellow, scrolled in black, falling off trains.

Rosie brought her yellow star, wrapped in a hankie,
to my father's funeral in Miami. So fragile she only
took it out for special occasions, but she let us hold it,
and it had a surprising weight, as though my father's soul
chose to linger there, as we remembered
his lucky breaks, from Poland to the Gulag,
then Uzbekistan, Germany, and the long road
to freedom, to America.

The day we hung the Jewish Star on Blanshard Street,
passers-by wondered what all the excitement was about.
"Look, we're Jews," I said, "and we're hanging our symbol
on our new building."

My throat constricts whenever we sing *Hatikva*,
that after two thousand years, we still haven't lost our hope,
and I always think of Ben Gurion
in the D.P. camps in Germany, where I was born,
declaring to those who had lost everything,
that *Eretz Yisrael* will be, again,
and I'm always in that crowd, under a blue
Mogen David, singing, through my tears
Od lo avdah tikvateynu—

Our hope is hung on Blanshard Street.

FOR ENRICA

1.

After the living have let her go
and her face has lost its sharpness
when my mind's eye seeks her out,
she will come to me, perhaps
when I'm pressing sweet-peas into earth
because I adore their fragrance, and hope
to fill my vases with them every summer,
and she'll remind me of the day we drank espressos
in her living room, and dabbed our lips
with crisp linen serviettes,
after the living have let her go

2.

After the living have let her go,
I will hear her tell me
that a rabbi must be someone whose hand
you can hold as you journey into death,
and I will see her unpack her little footstool
which she carried in her purse,
and unfold it in the pews,
where she roamed the desert with Moses,
or made promises to Naomi, like Ruth,
who also chose to be a Jew,
after the living have let her go

3.

After the living have let her go,
I will come to sit next to her,
with her sparkling *mots justes*
perfect for every occasion, like the time
I felt slighted and she taught me
those that don't want me don't deserve me
and I will record in a notebook all the other expressions
that elude me now as I recollect,
and we will smoke our secret cigarettes,
hers in a tortoise-shell holder,
after the living have let her go

4.

After the living have let her go,
I will remember how we greeted each other
with poems, in a room full of roses
and Florentine furniture, and
I will honor my word to keep writing
because words fed our hunger
like the *kreplach* and tortellini we had in our soup,
and having no children,
she feared being forgotten,
but I will remember her with *Kaddish*,
after the living have let her go

Pola, Last Visit

with one blind eye and
half a face she can't move
my aunt Pola chides
     don't look at me

fingers laced in hers,
I disobey

feel the warmth of her skin,
its stories

as I count the times
I've spent with her

my eye finds the postcard
she's kept
a painting from the Sargent show
I took her to
in Boston
she couldn't remember
the last time she'd been
to a museum

fifty-one years
in Kiriat Chaim,
never moved from the place
where she landed,
except from a tent to a
cinderblock flat

She tells me
at first they were
all kept together,
in 'Life Town',

        our own little ghetto of shame
where broken people
had to just get on with it,

        we had a country here to build

In an old picture
my cousins preen in her small garden
skirts pulled into wide smiles
fat bows in their hair

her garden
now grass
bleached, stubbly
prickles the eye

We the Exiled Sons of Eve in the Valley of Tears Greet You

my cousin Victor wrote, "but don't worry we have not lost our *joie de vivre.*"

Up on the Carmel in his sun-baked villa, 67 steps to reach his door. Such a beautiful ocean view he's spent many days admiring. Not the view he sees with the eyes in the back of his head, his Jewish head, his head filled with his parents' wars and his own; the Six-Day War, then '73, the wars of olive trees and bulldozers, the wars of I hate you for a hundred generations.

God soothed Abraham when he banished Hagar and Ishmael, giving them water and promises in the desert. Now the blood of Ishmael's sons is running in the streets and Israel's blood dries sticky on hands that wave while the whole world watches.

Potuach means open, as in "open your hand, O God, and deliver to all living things your joy", or as in the heart is open and a searing wind burns through it. Yehuda Amichai died that week, his last poem a plea for peace right now, while he still lived. *Sagour* means closed.

We went to bed on Saltspring watching stars through the skylight, "this same dome of night," I wrote Victor, "that shelters your mount of vineyards, and while waves lap up to your shoreline, I hear them here too. Same salt water, same earth, sky, same hearts open for the light of stars to pass through and rest us all in peace."

SEPTEMBER HARVEST

For weeks now
the island's been parched golden,
but bending close to earth,
I hear rumours of rain.

Yesterday you brought in the last figs
swollen with summer's nectar,
and a basket of tomatoes, your treasures.

I love the tastes you offer daily, that you
locate crab and rock cod as if
a vibration rises from opaque water,
and becomes sound, a whisper in your ear.
So it is in the forest, as you confide
with chanterelles and *cepes* under Douglas fir.
The kitchen is your pleasure temple, where
every evening is a prayer to earth's bounty,
to the fruit of vineyards, to burgundy glow.

After dinner, you stand quietly observing the stars,
and review what's caught in your mind's harvest.
Not much escapes your knowing, and the quickness
of your senses, not even an eagle,
when just a hint in the sky, or tonight,
the moist secrets of oysters.

Erotic Poem #1

When asked to choose a subject for this poem,
he said, please honey, not now, I'm shaving,
and she said, can't you shave and talk at the same
time? He made it clear that he didn't want
to bleed this morning, even though she said,
sweetheart, I like to be dominated, I want you
to tell me what you like,
you know how that works so well for me.
So he said, let me think about it,
as she took her tooth brush
into the other bathroom, because he was
still brushing on his lather, and already
running late. The mint swished its coolness
inside her mouth, as she looked in the mirror,
remembering how she loved him kissing
the back of her neck,
loved his breath nibbling her skin,
where her head joined the rest of her,
where she could never see.
She loved to offer this place up to him,
lowering her head, closing her eyes,
and waiting with complete
attention. Darling, you can have the shower
now, he whispered, his cheek
a waft of amber and sandalwood,
a mossy pillow in her nape.
I've been thinking of poppies, and arbutus.
Write about arbutus. Now there's a sexy tree.
O baby, o baby, she breathed,
arbutus, I wouldn't have thought arbutus.

Give me a moment, let me,
just let me imagine arbutus,
please baby, just blow once more,
here, yes here, let me,
just let me
write another poem.

DEATH TALK

I want to talk about death, register my annoyance
that this word has fallen out of favour.

What's wrong with death? It's clear and unequivocal.
Don't give me the wimpy 'passed' or 'passed over' or 'passed away'.
I want a strong and fearless word, worthy of tears.

I imagine the moment when death arrives
to change places with our bodies, what remains.
The things we touched, our gardens, whatever we created.
Oh and the weeping of those who love us, our spouses, our children,
our best friends, if they're lucky to be there to release us on our way.

I like hearing about these final moments, how, for instance,
Carol Shields listened to passages from *A Child In Time*,
or how Pierre Trudeau, with Margaret by his side,
listened to his favourite music and cried.
I'm grateful for these reports.

I think I would cry too, if I had that chance, when dying,
as I find partings difficult, and appreciate the benefits
a good cry brings.
What's beyond the tunnel, though? I'm very curious,
and imagine something extraordinary. After her mother died,
my friend Susan and I promised each other that we'll make contact
once there, and exchange notes. It always feels better, I find,
to have a prospect of adventure.

And yes, I'm afraid, of course I'm afraid, but I suspect we all fear
being born, too. Then look at us, obstinate revelers, begging
the party to keep on going, til the very last drop.

THE ROAD FROM ST. MICHAEL'S

Early morning walk, chewing on last night's dream, when barking dogs
scare me. OK, OK, I took a wrong turn, distracted by grasshoppers.
Their tiny drumsticks, fanning into green wings, fool me into thinking
they're butterflies. I'm new to Saskatchewan.

Gravel road bounding fields, grasshopper racket and rising heat
déjà-vu me. I'm seventeen, in Israel, just before the Six Day War.
We were kids, the state and me, growing up decently,
considering what we'd been through, before the years
of psychotherapy, before post-traumatic stress syndrome
had a name, before the intefadas, 9-11.

My dream kicks me in the head. A barge on wheels has to make a tight
manoeuvre down a very narrow road. It's dangerous cargo, but all I see
are giant cushions, as if this barge is a bed of woe, insisting its way
to an unknown destination, a mighty grief to comfort

while I'm just walking to Lumsden, to see the town I've landed in.
Soon an acrid smoke from burning tires heats up my head. I choose
to retreat to St. Michael's, now my refuge, and remember
(never did I think it possible in my own lifetime) Christians asking
my forgiveness, as the cross on the steeple pokes a hole
in the sun-bleached sky, and I yearn for blue, colour of spirit,
in Hebrew, *techelet*.

ISRAEL ON FIRE

I sit now listening to a voice older than time.
It rises from the bottom of a desert well,
a music as beautiful as the red sky I saw
one evening, caught in an ocean pool.
Red above, red below, while blue darkened
the edges, stained the surround.
My cousin's letter, telling me not to worry,
echoes back to me from his sun-baked home,
as I write from the sorrow in the well of my heart,
of hatred and killing that just won't stop, and
my fear of the beast that wants me dead,
my anger at this world still mad

Between the Doorposts

my eyes always reach
my hands always look
my thoughts always dart,
but I haven't yet learned the names,
not of the pale green moss
that droops like tattered banners
left out too long in the rain,
nor of the mottled lichen
that spreads its curly points
on the maple's bark,
nor of the leaf the colour
of cinnamon freshly peeled.
Not the dried brown fronds of fern,
or the wisps of golden grass
or the splay of broom,
I do not yet know their names.

I bind them with rosehips
to hang between my doorposts,
my talisman, mnemonic for
this world of wonders.

Utopia Parkway

His workshop crowded with hundreds of boxes
improbable sortings all labelled and filed
worlds older than the first midnight
I saw them in Chicago

improbable sortings all labelled and filed
scraps of his life released from sadness
I saw them in Chicago
a *coup de foudre* to jolt me on my way

scraps of his life released from sadness
parakeets on pedestals singing the hours
a *coup de foudre* to jolt me on my way
the boxmaker busy creating his worlds

parakeets on pedestals singing the hours
a box filled with Durer; trifles from the sea
the boxmaker busy creating his worlds
through a skyhole to Hotel du Nord

a box filled with Durer; trifles from the sea
worlds older than the first midnight
through a skyhole to Hotel du Nord
his workshop crowded with hundreds of boxes

Train of Thought

Sitting here relaxing on the grass, there's a copper grate planted by my feet. Pock-marked and rusty, scratched and soiled, it looks like a Hannelore Baron work of art. She's new to me, discovered when a friend gave me an old catalogue. A German Jew who managed to escape, but never could get over her fear. So she stayed in her room, her studio a table no bigger than a postage stamp, where she scratched and stitched and stained and pressed her way into creation. Out of rags and scraps she made such beauty it makes your heart twist just by looking.

Such beauty. So hidden. Emily Dickinson floats by in prim white, taking me to her tiny room, where I hear the nib of her pen scratching her exile into words.

I hear Sophie, in a New York library, asking, in Polish-accented broken English, for the poems of Emile Dickens. And the librarian says surely you mean Charles Dickens. But he wrote fiction, not poetry. And on she goes, humiliating Sophie, until Nathan overhears and comes to her rescue. He presents her with Emily Dickinson and off they go to a passion that cannot assuage their nightmares, no matter how much sex they try. And I'm amazed that I remember all this from so long ago, but *Sophie's Choice* is a story scratched deeply into my skin, and I bow down to William Styron for his monumental gift

and go down into Montreal's metro to find billboards announcing "Le Choix de Sophie". *Je me souviens* the moment I realize it's about shopping for clothes, when Sophie had to choose which one of her children to send to death, on the platform at Auschwitz, when they stepped off the train.

Pulling into Station Lionel Groulx, I'm sick of your story, Quebec, and your metro stations named after Nazi loving clerics and your unwillingness to admit your nasty past.

It's time to get up from the grass, and this copper grate that looks like a Hannelore Baron work of art.

CALLING

Listen. I'm calling the missing
I'm calling the wounded,
the frightened,
the ones with no face
I'm calling the mothers, the fathers
the sisters the brothers
I'm calling the *bubbies* the *zaides*
the aunts and the uncles
I'm calling the ones who have no graves
I'm calling the wives and the husbands
the beaten, the broken,
the burnt and the frozen,
the buried alive
I'm calling the soldiers
who died in the battles
I'm calling the rivers the oceans
the wind and the rain
I'm calling the birds of the forest
the wolves of the mountains
I'm calling the wicked, the thirsty
the gifted, the lousy
the outcasts
the sorry
I'm calling

I'm calling

What She Wants

She wants time. Clear space. She wants to go to Umbria for a long holiday, then keep going. She longs to give up her identity as a health care worker. She wants to sit down at her desk everyday and knock out pages, at least five, every day. Or one poem. One poem a day. She wants a book. A published work. A shitty little novel. She wants to go to India and not be afraid of the crowds and poverty and misery and dirt. She wants to be at ease travelling after September 11th. She wants to bellydance. She wants to sing. She wants a show. She's an artist. She wants to read all the books in her bookcases. Have her salon. She yearns to find the wherewithall to do her yoga every day. Have a cabin to retreat to. Sit by a fire.

She wants to put her life in her pocket, keep it in reserve, like a tissue, just in case, because it's a very good life, desirable, valuable, privileged, but she remembers how she was wild once, and she wants to taste that again— the adventure, the thrill of new, of risking, of going out on a limb, like Paul Simon's tumbler/acrobat that he sings about on the road to Memphis Tennessee.

Where did those years disappear, the kid years, the toil years, the tear years. She's over the childhoods, has adults for children, they survived. Now new life fills her days and she clears the sink and the counters more, and the toys, and she's prickly about clutter, downright intolerant, because she wants to run away from home, because it weighs down her chest and ties her hands and occupies her thoughts. And time itself is a loud ticking and her bones are weakening and she's getting older and she still wants to have a go at making it, at getting it out of her, and feeding herself all she longs to taste yet, and wrap her arms around. She's been a good good girl and now she wants to be selfish. Yes good and selfish.

VALENTINE

tonight in our bed
my head rests on your pillow, your hand
cups my breast
darling listen to our hearts
chirping like sparrows

Blessings in Praise of Life and Its Creator

a found poem from Gates of the House,
The New Union Home Prayerbook

over bread
over wine
over pastry
over fruits that grow on trees
over fruits and vegetables that grow in the soil
on an occasion of joy
on seeing lightning or other natural wonders
on hearing thunder
on seeing the ocean
on seeing the beauties of nature
on seeing a rainbow
on seeing trees in blossom
on seeing a great Torah scholar
upon recovery from serious illness
or upon escape from danger
before a journey
on hearing of the death of a dear one
on hearing good tidings

This Cream Cheese Is As Old As The War In Iraq

for Daniel

Eleven days ago I bought it, that Wednesday
in March. How ridiculous to keep track of a war
by the age of my cream cheese, but I do,
when I open the fridge, and remember
that I was spreading cream cheese on bread,
making cucumber sandwiches,
garnished with pimento, olives and parsley,
to offer my guests, while I worried about
your disappearance, in Montreal,
trying to imagine why no one had heard from you
for forty-eight hours, while

you knew nothing of the commotion you'd caused,
nor the worry I fed my guests,
along with poetry and cucumber sandwiches,
or their reassurance that you were twenty-one
and probably screwing your brains out somewhere.

That night the bombs fell on Baghdad, you surfaced
as predicted, and now, eleven days later, the left-over
cream cheese, still fresh in its package, I take out and
spread on my bagel, and sit with a coffee, reading the news.

Two brothers, just kids, conscripted in Baghdad
and shipped off to Basra under threat of death.
They hid for a week with no food or water, when
overtaken by misery, surrendered to the first
foreigners they happened to see. The journalists
were willing to send word to their parents,
but the boys changed their minds, fearful
the news could have them killed.

I sob for those boys and their parents,
sickened by Saddam, I want him dead. I want
this war to end as favourably as your disappearance,
and I want them as lucky as we are, in freedom,
and please please let it be quick. As quick as the date
my cream cheese expires. That would be early next week.

Maimonides Girl:
A Few Words About My Monoprints

Strips of paper, side by side,
above / below.
Parallel worlds, separated,
connected by line, thread,

                    by yearning.

By accident or design.

Biblical stories still resonate:
Sarah and Hagar.
Ishmael and Isaac.
Jew, Christian, Muslim,
we all know them.
We are their children.

Israel and Palestine,
The Dome of the Rock sits atop
the Holy Temple.
If I forget thee, Jerusalem, may I forget my right hand
never forget, our Jewish mantra
forgetthepast.com: my niece's peace plan
with my right hand I write *shalom*

Hands pull threads to make the curtain
for the holy ark,
crowned by the the ten commandments.
Hands embroider dresses for the holy body,
but you musn't show the body,
no graven images, no human or animal forms

You must decapitate animals and make them look like flowers,
said Ibn Abbas, to the painter; only God can create life.
Welcome to iconophobia, see
what's left of the twin towers

Stone, wood, fire,
houses of prayer.

I never even saw a picture of Isaac,
my grandfather,
until a surprise discovery
three years ago, in my aunt Pola's house,
in Haifa: a photograph
with his own handwriting on the back.
Felt like I'd unearthed a lost continent.

See the Cohen's fingers splayed
to transmit God's blessings,
on abandoned tombstones.
My father passed his Cohen status on to me
but we have no graves
for our grandparents,
aunts, uncles and cousins.
It's up to me to tell you
they lived and loved

Here is my mother's story:
She the twin who survived.
Here is my father's story:
He kept his silence til the end.

Here are my stories.

The work of my hands.

TRANSPLANT

The little dog refuses to leave the body
of his murdered master, whose face we cannot see
in the photograph from Zimbabwe.
I huddle in the corpse of my lost world

plucked from the carnage,
transplanted like a kidney or a lung,
I live in another body, another
continent but remember

the sounds of wind and river,
churn of mill stone grinding wheat
the heat produced by taproots
as they burrow through shale
and stone

EVIDENCE OF THE EXISTENCE OF GOD IN MY KITCHEN CATCH-ALL DRAWER

Here is chaos, the beginning of God's story,
retold every day in this slide of wood.
Here live the things that hold the world together,
the hooks and the wires, the tape and the glue.
Here lie screwdrivers with their swollen handles,
filled with interchangeable endings,
like flowers with many stamens.
And clippers and scissors, wrenches and pliers,
with their curved or pointed noses,
each designed for a particular assignment,
like the beaks of finches, to match their seeds.
Here seed packets wait for their planting,
knowing their time will come, and scattered amongst them,
little bags of things that had a purpose, once,
but the apocrypha of these small mysteries
was never written. Here beats a constant faith,
that someday their meaning will be revealed.
Here the miracle of light is ever ready,
for the birthdays, and feast days, and the seventh day,
when God took a rest. And buried under it all,
the last dog's leash and collar, reminding us
that three letters can spell a multitude of words,
and that our days are numbered. Let's sing their praises.

NOTES

p.22 Mama, Isaac and Me
 chumash: a Hebrew word for the Five Books of Moses, derive
  from *chamesh*, the number five
 eretz hakodesh: Hebrew, The Holy Land
 Yitzhak: Hebrew, for Isaac
 Numah b'ni: literally, "sleep, my son," a Hebrew lullaby

p.24 Family History
 yitgadal veyitkadash shemay rabah: opening words of
  the Mourner's Kaddish prayer
 Make me a channel of your peace...:
  from the Prayer of St. Francis

p.31 My Life in Theatre
 chambre de bonne: maid's room

p.35 Wet Dog Day
 nobody stuffs the world in at your eyes, from "Snow"
  by Margaret Avison

p.36 D.T.G.
  last line a quotation from "Great Dog Poem No. 2"
  by Mark Strand

p.47 Waking Up
 *I would like to give you the silver branch, the small white
  flower* from "Variation on the Word Sleep"
  by Margaret Atwood

p.49 Hanging the Star of David on Blanshard Street
 Mogen David: Hebrew/Yiddish: literally, David's Shield
  or Star of David
 od lo avdah tikvateynu: Hebrew, from Israel's national
  anthem *Hatikva*, "we still haven't lost our hope,"

ACKNOWLEDGEMENTS

Some of these poems have appeared in *The Malahat Review, Arc, Other Voices,* the anthologies *Moving Small Stones* and *Masks* edited by Patrick Lane, and in *Seven Fat Years,* a letterpress chapbook published by Frog Hollow Press, 2002.

So many people have helped me create this book. I thank Dan Bar-On, who first heard my stories at the 'Bereavement as Healing' conference in Montreal in 1994, and urged me to publish them. I chose poetry.

I could not have become a poet without the guidance of my teachers: Patrick Lane, Marge Piercy, Don McKay, Lorna Crozier, Patricia Young, Jay Ruzesky, Betsy Warland, Jim Bertolino, and Sheri-D Wilson. Many of the poems in this collection began from seeds planted and nurtured in their workshops. I am deeply grateful for their generous gifts to me.

My gratitude also extends to a community of poets and writing companions who, over the years, have encouraged, inspired and listened so critically: Enrica Glickman (of blessed memory), Nicholas Cohen, Laurie Elmquist, Marlene Grand Maitre, Fran Backhouse, Elliot Gose, Susan Stenson, Dvora Levin, Rhonda Batchelor, Diane Buchanan, Dave Margoshes, and above all, Wendy Morton, who believed in the significance of this book.

I especially thank Patrick Lane, who told me that he loved my voice, and taught me to trust it.

And always, Robert McConnell.